I0122100

The Stepmom's Boundary Blueprint

Your All-in-One Workbook, Journal & Coloring Book

*Reclaim your time, energy
and peace without guilt!*

BY CLAUDETTE CHENEVERT

The Stepmom's Boundary Blueprint: Your All-in-One Workbook & Coloring Book
By Claudette Chenevert

Edited by Christine G. Adamo, dba "A-ha!" Creative
Original cover art by Claudette Chenevert
Interior sketches courtesy of Depositphotos.com
Front cover layout & design by Christine G. Adamo
Back cover design & photography by Claudette Chenevert

Print ISBN: 978-1-7336465-3-6
Library of Congress Control Number: 2025910240
Printed in the United States of America

DEDICATION

To every stepmom who has ever felt obliged to say "yes" when her heart and mind screamed "No!" this journal is for you. To the stepmom who gives endlessly—often at her own expense—may these pages remind you: *Your needs matter, too!*

CONTENTS

ACKNOWLEDGEMENTS

To all the courageous stepmoms who've generously shared their journeys, experiences and wisdom with me over time: *Thank you!* Your openness, honesty and vulnerability have deeply enriched this work. Your resilience in navigating the many complexities of stepfamily life is a beacon of hope for others. I'm continually inspired by your strength and hope that this journal serves as a supportive guide on your path ahead.

To my family: *Thank you!* Your patience and understanding, even when my focus has been consumed by projects like this one, is unwavering. It's you who reminds me to practice what I teach, especially when I stumble. You encourage me to pause, reflect and continue growing. I'm grateful for your presence in my life and the life we've built together—imperfections and all.

To those who've supported me through this process, whether with feedback, guidance or simply believing in the importance of this work: *Thank you!* Your encouragement has been the push I needed to bring this journal to life. I truly appreciate every nudge, insight and reminder to keep going.

PREFACE

The life of a stepmom is filled with EXPECTATIONS, COMPLEXITIES and EMOTIONS others may never fully understand. As a result, our experience can be isolating, frustrating and filled with self-doubt.

Still, I want you to know this: *You're not alone!* Many stepmoms I've met, become friends with and/or coached all face the same challenges. Sure, some are unique to their circumstances but we have a lot in common. That's why I believe that together we can begin to redefine what it means to show up for ourselves without experiencing guilt yet still showing up for our families.

The Stepmom's Boundary Blueprint is a SAFE, JUDGMENT-FREE SPACE where you get to explore your hopes, dreams and worries. In self-reflection and through "Time to Flourish" boundary-setting exercises, you'll: Reclaim your voice, honor your emotions and step into your confidence. With every step, I encourage you to play, doodle and color inside and outside the lines.

Leave your mark on this journal and your heart. Take notes that document this heroic journey you're on. I left plenty of space for you to explore. Be sure to remember that prioritizing your well-being and setting healthy boundaries aren't selfish acts. They're essential to honoring your needs and limits. Protect your peace and build a healthier, more fulfilling life for all of you.

Compassionately,

Claudette
@TheStepmomCoach
Claudette@StepmomCoach.com

Welcome: How to Use This Journal

Stepmom life is not for the faint of heart. You're balancing emotions, relationships and expectations that often feel like they're pulling you in every direction at once. You're managing messy dynamics between yourself, your partner, your stepchildren and sometimes even the kids' other parent. Some days are filled with joy, laughter and connection. Others bring conflict, misunderstanding and feelings of isolation. No wonder it's so easy to lose sight of your needs and well-being.

This journal is your sanctuary—a safe haven where you can be honest with yourself and explore your thoughts and feelings without judgment. It's a place to pause, breathe and reconnect with your inner self. In addition, each section of this journal offers insights, exercises and journal prompts to guide you through the process of setting better boundaries. Boundaries aren't walls, by the way. They're doors that allow healthier and more fulfilling relationships to thrive.

Our goal is to make sure you become better able and equipped to:

- ♡ Identify areas where boundaries are missing or weak.
- ♡ Develop clear and compassionate ways of setting limits.
- ♡ Hold firm to your boundaries, even when met with resistance.
- ♡ Confidently prioritize your well-being as you grow your relationships.

This journal is here to support you every step of the way!

What follows are my tips for making the most of *The Stepmom's Boundary Blueprint* all-in-one workbook, journal and coloring book experience.

✓ **Move through the sections at your own pace—knowing there's no rush.**
Boundaries take time to build and strengthen. Some sections may resonate with you immediately. Others may feel challenging. Give yourself permission to take breaks, skip ahead, revisit topics and go at a pace that's right for you.

✓ **Use reflection prompts to explore your experiences with boundaries.**
The journal reflections exercises I've included are designed to help you uncover where your boundaries are strong and where they could use some reinforcement. So, be honest with yourself. And keep in mind that all of your experiences, feelings and struggles are 100% valid.

✓ **Test boundary setting and reinforcement exercises in all areas of life.**
Boundaries aren't simply concepts we need to understand. They require action! Each exercise in this journal will help you put ideas into practice, so that you can begin to communicate your limits and uphold them confidently.

✓ **Revisit sections as your boundaries evolve and circumstances change.**
What works for you today may not work six months from now. As situations and relationships shift, so will your boundaries. Use this journal as an ongoing resource to check in with yourself and make adjustments when needed.

✓ **Be patient and compassionate with yourself. This is a learning process!**
Setting and maintaining boundaries is a skill that takes time to develop. You may face resistance from others or even from yourself. Mistakes and setbacks are part of the journey. Treat yourself with kindness at every turn of the page.

✓ **Acknowledge yourself for showing up for yourself.** Whether you write a few sentences here and there or fill every page available, the most important thing is that you show up for yourself. Why? Because every step you take in honoring your boundaries is a step toward greater peace, confidence and well-being.

PERMISSION SLIPS:

Sprinkled throughout your workbook you'll find "permission slips" like the sticky note below. They're meant to encourage you to pause, note how you truly feel (i.e., anxious, pissed off, relieved) and then acknowledge that versus pretend as if everything's okay.

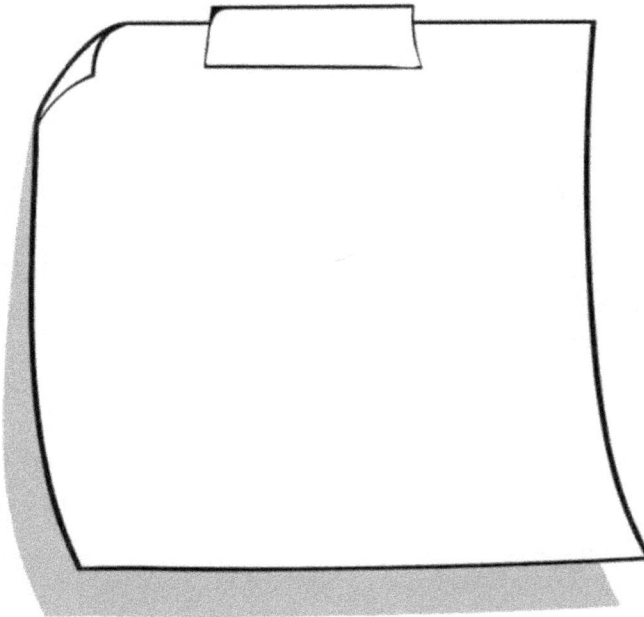

How do you feel right now? Whatever's going on, jot it down! Permission slips give you 100% freedom from self-censoring and pretending.

Download additional permission slips online:
https://www.StepmomCoach.com/Boundaries-Workbook-Bonus

Why Permission Slips Matter

Sometimes the hardest part of setting boundaries isn't saying "no" to others. It's saying "yes" to yourself! As a stepmom, you might feel pressure to stay strong, always be agreeable or hide how you truly feel.

You tell yourself you "should" be over it by now or that your emotions aren't valid. Well, here's the truth: You're allowed to feel ALL of it: the guilt, the fear, the frustration. Even the desire to step back (or away) and breathe a minute.

That's where permission slips come in. Each is a simple statement of fact. But it gives you the internal validation you need and deserve in difficult moments. It's a powerful reminder that your feelings are real—and that you don't need anyone else's approval for your truth to be honored and understood.

Other Uses for Permission Slips

Anytime you feel stuck, overwhelmed or unsure about how to respond to a situation, search your journal for a permission slip (or blank reflection page). Write down what you're feeling and why. No need to sugarcoat it. This is your journal! For example, "I'm so mad at the ex right now for showing up here!"

I find permission slips especially helpful when I'm navigating guilt, doing way too much people-pleasing or dealing with a lot of internal chatter. Maybe the stepkids are in a mood. Or I don't feel like enforcing boundaries today. Or a boundary's been crossed for the hundredth time and I'm fuming mad.

Let your healing begin—with kindness, honesty and permission to be 100% human! Write down how you think it'll feel to face your truth without worry:

Try This: Write your own permission slip for something that's been weighing on you lately. What is it you need to allow yourself to feel? Or to do? Or to say here, in private, without having to worry about anyone's feelings being hurt?

"Today, I finally give myself permission to ..."

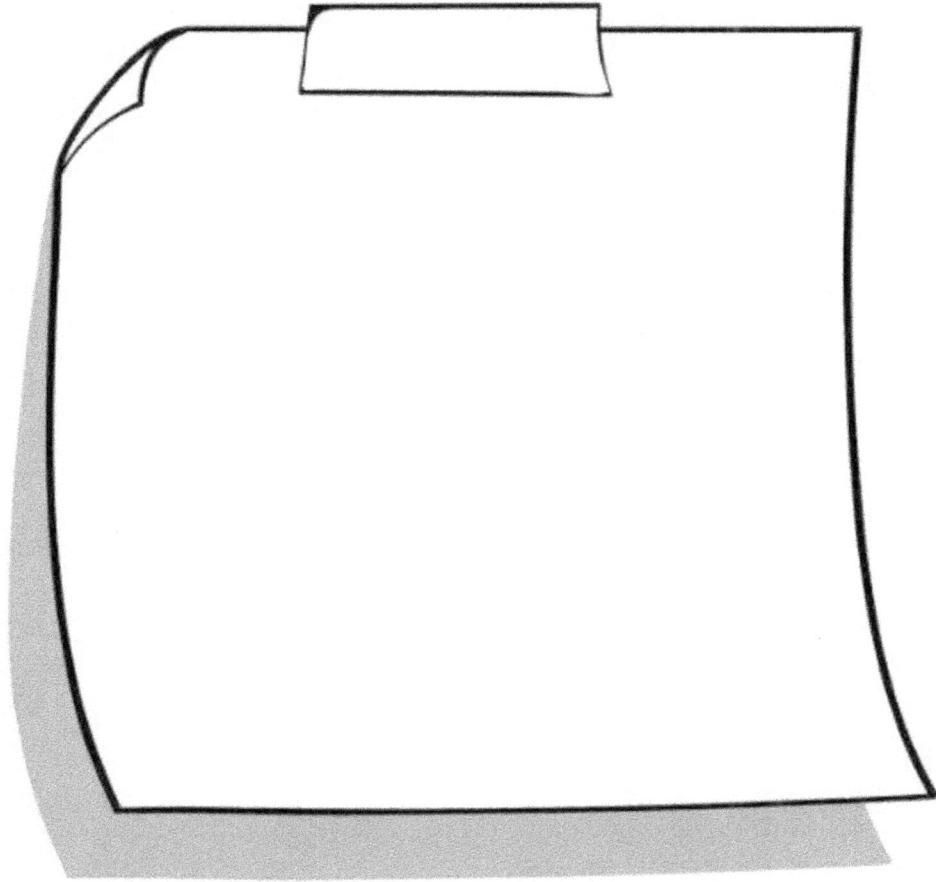

Remember: Most stepmoms have similar stories to tell—but yours is still unique to you. Take a deep breath in. Let it out slowly. Acknowledge how brave you are for undertaking this journey of self-care and self-discovery.

Section 1

Understanding Boundaries

"Daring to set boundaries is about having the courage to love ourselves, even when we risk disappointing others."

— Brené Brown

What Boundaries Are
—& Why They Matter

*B*oundaries are essential guidelines which help us to protect our emotional, mental and physical well-being. They serve as invisible lines that define what we're willing to accept and tolerate from others—and what we're not. By setting and maintaining clear boundaries, what we do is create a sense of safety for ourselves and ensure that we have comfortable levels of autonomy in our relationships and daily lives.

Why Boundaries Matter

Boundaries aren't for shutting people out or being rigid. They're essential to self-respect, balance and healthier interactions. Healthy boundaries help us:

♡ *Maintain healthy relationships.* Boundaries teach others how to treat us so that we receive respect and consideration.

♡ *Protect your well-being.* Without clear boundaries in place, we risk emotional exhaustion, resentment and burnout.

♡ *Honor your values and needs.* Setting boundaries ensures that actions we take align nicely with our personal priorities.

♡ *Reduce stress and overwhelm.* When we communicate our limits, we prevent situations that drain our energy.

Boundaries in Stepfamily Life

As a stepmom, boundary-setting can feel like an especially complex process. You may feel pressure to take on responsibilities which don't align with your role or your personal values. You may struggle with where to draw the line in relation to parenting, household expectations or interactions with extended family. Without both having and communicating clear boundaries, you risk feeling lost and getting buried under other people's expectations of you. This typically leads to frustration, guilt and/or resentment.

Boundaries Are Flexible

A common misconception is that boundaries must be rigid. In reality, you may want to shift them depending on factors like current circumstances, relationship ease or strain and recent wins or personal growth. What matters is that your boundaries what's healthiest for you at any given time. Some may need to be firm, while others might allow for flexibility and adaptation.

Remember: Give yourself "permission" to process how you feel at any given moment. For example, "I hate that I struggle to reinforce boundaries!"

Types of Boundaries

There are many different kinds of boundaries: emotional, physical, time specific, communication, parental and more. Knowing which different types of boundaries exist will help you to:

♡ **Pinpoint trouble areas.** You may find that one particular boundary or type of boundary is crossed often, while others are usually respected.

♡ **Improve communication.** Being able to express which boundary was crossed will help others understand and meet your needs better.

♡ **Increase self-awareness.** Better understanding your limits in different areas will show you where you need to strengthen your boundaries.

♡ **Make intentional choices.** Identifying boundary types lets you choose where to focus your effort first based on your priorities.

Next we'll consider and reflect on several types of boundaries worth setting.

EMOTIONAL BOUNDARIES

Protecting Your Feelings & Energy

Emotional boundaries involve recognizing and expressing your feelings without fear of judgment or invalidation. They help you separate your own emotions from those of others, ensuring that you don't mistakenly take on their burdens or allow them to manipulate your feelings. Setting emotional boundaries allows you to maintain your well-being and prevent emotional exhaustion.

Examples:

♡ Say "no" to requests that make you uncomfortable or drain your energy.

♡ Choose not to engage in conversations that trigger you emotionally.

♡ Limit contact with people who constantly disrespect your feelings.

♡ Express your own needs and expectations clearly and assertively.

Journal Reflection:

How do I usually react when someone oversteps my emotional boundaries?

What's ONE emotional boundary I struggle to enforce? Why is that?

How do I feel when I set an emotional boundary? What fears or anxieties come up for me?

Think of a recent situation that felt you feeling drained emotionally. How might setting a boundary have changed the experience?

What's ONE emotional boundary I'll commit to strengthening this week?

PHYSICAL BOUNDARIES

Defining Personal Space & Comfort

Physical boundaries help to define your personal space, body autonomy and comfort with physical touch and interpersonal interactions. These specific kinds of boundaries help you determine and explain how close others are allowed to be/get, who's allowed to reach out and touch you and what levels of access others have to your belongings or physical presence.

Examples:

- ♡ Decide who is/isn't allowed to hug you.
- ♡ Ask for space to yourself whenever you need it.
- ♡ Experiment with face-to-face distance in social settings.
- ♡ If you don't feel comfortable sharing personal belongings, say so.

Journal Reflection:

When was a time in which I felt as if my physical boundaries were being disrespected? How did I respond?

Do I struggle to ask for personal space? If so, why? If no, why not?

How can I communicate my physical boundaries in a clear, respectful way?

What's ONE small way I'll reinforce my physical boundaries this week?

How does it feel if someone respects my personal space and boundaries?

TIME BOUNDARIES

Managing Availability & Prioritizing Your Time

Time boundaries involve being intentional about how you spend your time. You want to ensure that you're not overcommitting yourself and that you're not allowing others to dictate your schedule. These boundaries help you to prioritize what truly matters while protecting your energy from unnecessary or unpleasant obligations.

Examples:

- ♡ Schedule time for self-care and personal pursuits.
- ♡ Delegate tasks and responsibilities whenever possible.
- ♡ Limit time spent on social media or with other distractions.
- ♡ Say "no" to that new task whether you're busy or not interested.

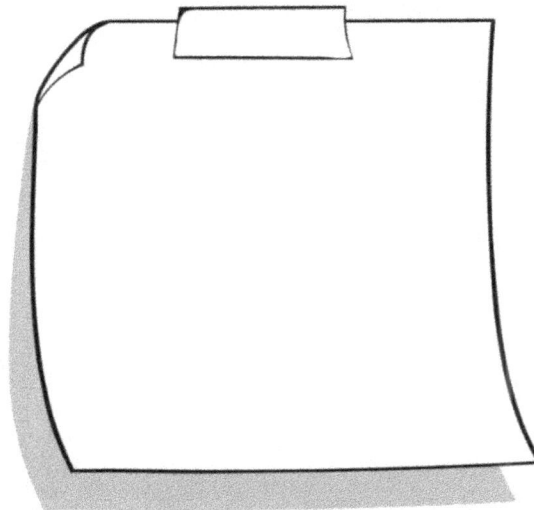

Journal Reflection:

How do I currently prioritize my time? Where do I feel stretched too thin?

What's ONE commitment I've taken on that no longer serves me? Why?

How can I communicate my time boundaries to others without guilt?

What's ONE way I will commit to reclaiming time for myself this week?

How does protecting my time improve my mental + emotional well-being?

COMMUNICATION BOUNDARIES

Determine What Conversations & Interactions Are Acceptable

Communication boundaries help you to set limits on types of conversations you engage in as well as any ways in which you allow others to speak to you. Not to mention who you allow to speak with you and when! These types of boundaries ensure that you're spoken to with respect and that you don't get drawn into discussions that are toxic, unproductive or emotionally draining.

Examples:

- ♡ I will not engage in gossip or negative talk.
- ♡ I will avoid disrespectful/offensive conversations.
- ♡ I will speak up when I'm being interrupted or talked over.
- ♡ I will bow out of conversations I find draining or unproductive.
- ♡ I will limit when and how others contact me (i.e., text only, workdays).

Journal Reflection:

Which or what kinds of conversations tend to leave me feeling drained, frustrated and/or disrespected? And why is that?

Have I ever stayed silent when I wanted to set a communication boundary? What stopped me? And what's ONE way I might overcome that?

How can I assert my boundaries in conversations without feeling guilty?

What's ONE small communication boundary I will put in place this week?

How do I feel when someone honors my communication boundaries? Why?

PARENTAL BOUNDARIES

Clarify Your Role & Define Expectations

Parental boundaries help to establish clarity around your stepparent role. They also help to ensure that expectations are discussed, understood and accepted by each adult with a say in how your stepfamily functions. When these boundaries are lacking, stepparents tend to feel easily overwhelmed.

Without parental boundaries, overstepping can occur. Tensions can build between family members and households. Ideally, setting and maintaining these boundaries makes room for a more harmonious stepfamily dynamic in which each adult who fills a role is understood and respected.

Examples:

♡ Discuss discipline strategies with your partner and then establish a united front in support of those.

♡ Respect and support relationships among and between stepchildren and their respective parents.

♡ Foster unique bonds with those stepkids without trying to replace, compete with or alienate other key adult figures in their lives.

♡ Set and communicate clear expectations for behavior (i.e., the kids', the ex's), making sure to enforce consequences consistently.

♡ Seek out support or guidance from therapists, coaches and others with deep knowledge of stepfamily dynamics and stepparent challenges.

♡ Learn to recognize when it's best and healthiest to step back and let the children's parents handle certain situations.

Journal Reflection:

How do I define my role as a stepparent? Does this align with my partner's expectations?

What parental boundaries do I struggle with the most? Why?

How do I currently handle situations in which my boundaries, as the kids' stepparent, are either ignored or challenged?

What's ONE step I will take this week to communicate my boundaries more clearly to my partner? And maybe even my stepchildren?

How does respecting my own boundaries, as a stepparent and a partner in a stepcouple, improve my relationships with my stepkids and my partner?

ADDITIONAL BOUNDARIES

Keep in mind that boundaries are guidelines we set in order to to protect our emotional, mental and physical well-being. They're meant to enhance your sense of safety in all areas. Additional types of boundaries include:

- ♡ **Financial:** Set limits on financial contributions and shared expenses.
- ♡ **Digital:** Manage online interactions and social media engagement.
- ♡ **Work:** Strike a healthy balance, limiting work hours/responsibilities.
- ♡ **Spiritual:** Guard your beliefs and values versus compromise them.
- ♡ **Intellectual:** Respect differing opinions and perspectives without feeling obligated to abandon, change or modify your own.

Journal Reflection:

Where in my life do I struggle most with boundaries? Why is that?

In what other areas of my life do I want to begin setting boundaries?

Remember: Setting boundaries is an ongoing process that takes practice, time and self-reflection. Be patient with yourself and others as you begin to establish more healthy boundaries in relationships at home, at work, etc.

Section 2

Honoring Your Limits

*"Self-care is
how you take your
power back."*

— Lalah Delia

Why It's Okay to Take Care of Yourself

Setting boundaries, as a stepmom especially, is one of the most important and transformative things you'll ever do for your well-being. Yet it can also feel like one of the hardest. The expectations placed on you—by a partner, stepkids, extended family and even society—make it difficult to define where your responsibilities end ... and you own individual needs begin.

By making time to reflect on and care for your mental health, you're not only supporting yourself. You're building greater resilience, cultivating self-compassion and modeling the importance of self-care for everyone around you. You're showing your partner, your children (if you have them) and your stepkids that prioritizing your well-being isn't simply okay but necessary.

The benefits of setting boundaries are many and include the following:

- ♡ **Improved self-esteem and self-respect:** Setting boundaries shows that you respect yourself and your needs.

- ♡ **Reduced stress and anxiety:** Setting boundaries helps to reduce stress and overwhelm by preventing you from taking on too much.

- ♡ **Healthier relationships:** Setting boundaries helps you to build much healthier and more respectful relationships with others.

- ♡ **Increased control and autonomy:** Setting, communicating and then enforcing boundaries teaches others what you will and won't allow.

- ♡ **Greater emotional and physical well-being:** Boundaries improve overall well-being by reserving time, space and energy for what matters most to you.

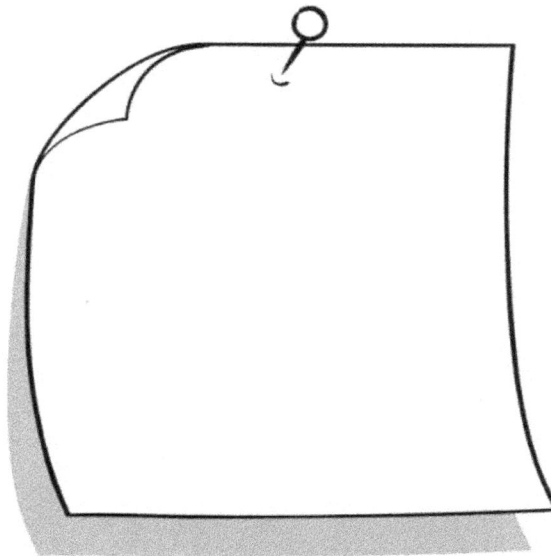

Journal Reflection:

How do I feel when someone disregards my boundaries?

How might setting boundaries help me be more present, patient and loving in interactions with my partner, my stepkids and others?

Practice Saying No

*I*t's okay to intentionally decline engagements which are likely to deplete your energy, overextend your capabilities and/or impose emotional burdens that aren't your responsibility to deal with. This includes saying "no" to:

♡ **Conversations that will drain you:** These might be interactions that tend to leave you feeling emotionally exhausted, stressed or simply overwhelmed. They could involve negative people, contentious topics or discussions that don't align with your values or interests.

♡ **Activities you don't have the capacity for:** This encompasses tasks or commitments which exceed your available time, your energy and your resources. It's important to recognize your limits always and to avoid overextending yourself—or you risk burn out and frustration.

♡ **Emotional labor that's not yours to carry:** This refers to any type or level of emotional support, caretaking or problem-solving you may be asked to provide for others. While empathy and support are valuable traits, it's essential that you set boundaries which help you to avoid taking on emotional burdens that aren't your responsibility.

Journal Reflection:

What's ONE area where I wish I could say "no" more often?

What's ONE thing I'll say "no" to this week? What other specific examples come to mind? (Put a star next to any you consider Top Priority.)

Boundary Scripts

*R*emember that saying no is a way of protecting your own well-being and preserving your energy for things that truly matter. Preserve and protect your time, energy and peace of mind more easily by creating scripts for yourself that feel authentic and become part of your vocabulary.

Examples:

- ✓ "I appreciate that you thought of me but I can take that on right now."

- ✓ "I'm not in a position to commit myself to anything else."

- ✓ "I understand that you're going through a difficult time. I'm just not equipped to provide the support you need."

Time to Flourish: The Power of 'No'

This exercise is meant to help you practice saying "no" with confidence and conviction. Each prompt applies to a range of different situations. Make one of them your go-to. Or use the space below to brainstorm a few others.

Complete EACH sentence in a way that feels natural to you:

♡ "I appreciate the offer but won't be able to _____."

♡ "I know this is important to you but I need to prioritize _____."

♡ "I understand your perspective but made my decision to _____."

Journal Reflection:

Which example of saying "no" felt the hardest for me? Why is that?

How could I make that statement feel more authentic or comfortable?

Fear of Saying No

There are many reasons why you might be afraid to say "no," including:

♡ **Fear of Missing Out (FOMO):** Do you say "yes" to things because you're afraid of missing out? Remind yourself that you can't do everything. And it's better to miss out on some things if it means that you get to prioritize your own well-being.

♡ **People-Pleasing:** Do you say "yes" to things because you want to please others, even if it comes at the expense of your own needs? I'm sure you know by now that you can't please everyone. Putting your own needs and well-being first is a must.

♡ **Guilt & Obligation:** Do you say "yes" to things just because you feel guilty or obligated? Even though you know you don't want to do them? You have the right to say "no" without guilt or apology.

♡ **Skewed Self-Worth:** Self-worth is not determined by how much you do for others. Commit that to memory. You're 100% worthy of love and respect regardless of how much you give to others.

Time to Flourish: Identify & Reframe Boundary Fears

Many stepmoms hesitate to set boundaries because of fear: fear of rejection, conflict or guilt. Let's work through that, identifying and reframing yours.

STEP 1: Identify ONE boundary you struggle to set.

STEP 2: What fear comes up when you think about setting this boundary?

STEP 3: Clearly name and then reframe that fear. Say you think: "If I set this boundary, they'll be upset with me." Try: "Setting this boundary allows me to take care of me first. I then get to foster healthier relationships as a result."

Now it's your turn!

Journal Reflection:

How did that reframe change how I feel about enforcing this boundary?

Assessing Your Current Boundaries

aking time to identify what your current boundaries are gives you the information you need to move forward confidently. When you skip taking time to evaluate where you're at, it becomes easy to let unhealthy patterns take over and continue to derail your best efforts. Any areas of stepfamily life that make you feel uncomfortable, overwhelmed, guilty or drained requires your IMMEDIATE attention.

Time to Flourish: Inventory Your Boundaries

Take a moment to assess your current boundaries in different areas of your life and role as a stepmom. Rate your boundaries in each category below on a Scale of 1 to 5 where 1 = None, 3 = Some and 5 = Strong/clear boundaries.

♡ _____ Personal Time

♡ _____ Couple's Relationship

♡ _____ Step-/Parenting

♡ _____ Emotional Space

♡ _____ Work/Life Balance

♡ _____ Extended Family

♡ _____ Social Commitments

Journal Reflection:

Which area do I feel the most confident in? What's the reason for that?

Which area needs the most improvement? What are some likely reasons?

What's ONE step I'll take to start strengthening my weakest boundary area?

Identifying Areas
of Overcommitment

Take time to list out some current commitments and obligations. Think about where you see patterns of discomfort or overwhelm.

Journal Reflection:

Where am I saying "yes" out of obligation, guilt or a sense of duty despite my inner voice screaming "NO!" loudly enough that I can't miss it?

Which specific tasks, activities and/or social engagements really drain my energy and leave me feeling resentful?

How will setting boundaries in those specific areas impact my well-being, my relationships and my sense of control or self-agency?

Setting Healthy Boundaries

Once you've identified areas where you're overcommitting, you'll want to prioritize setting healthy boundaries. This means learning to say "no" without guilt or apology, recognizing that your own needs and well-being are important and communicating limits clearly and assertively.

Say "no" to yet another social invitation. Delegate a task at work or at home. Set limits on your availability in general. The many happy side effects will include feeling less burdened and feeling brave enough to keep openly communicating your needs to your partner, the kids, friends, colleagues, etc.

Journal Reflection:

What's ONE specific boundary I will create this week on the path to reclaiming my peace and protecting my energy?

Remember: Setting boundaries is an act of self-love and self-respect.

Additional Tips

Remind yourself that setting boundaries is an ongoing process. With time and practice, you'll learn to say "no" without guilt and to prioritize your own needs. The time and effort you invest in you are worth it. By setting healthy boundaries, you set yourself up to reclaim your inner peace, preserve your energy and live a more fulfilling life. Here are other steps you can take:

- ➢ **Practice self-awareness.** Pay attention to your body and emotions to recognize when you're feeling drained or overwhelmed.

- ➢ **Prioritize self-care.** Make time for activities that recharge and nourish you: exercise, relaxation, nature hikes, spending time with friends, etc.

- ➢ **Communicate assertively.** Get really good at expressing your needs and boundaries to others while being clear and respectful.

- ➢ **Don't feel guilty.** Remember that you always have the right to say "no"—without feeling guilty or obligated to explain yourself.

- ➢ **Seek support.** If you're struggling to set boundaries or to manage emotional labor, consider the support of qualified coach or counselor.

Section 3

Family Boundaries

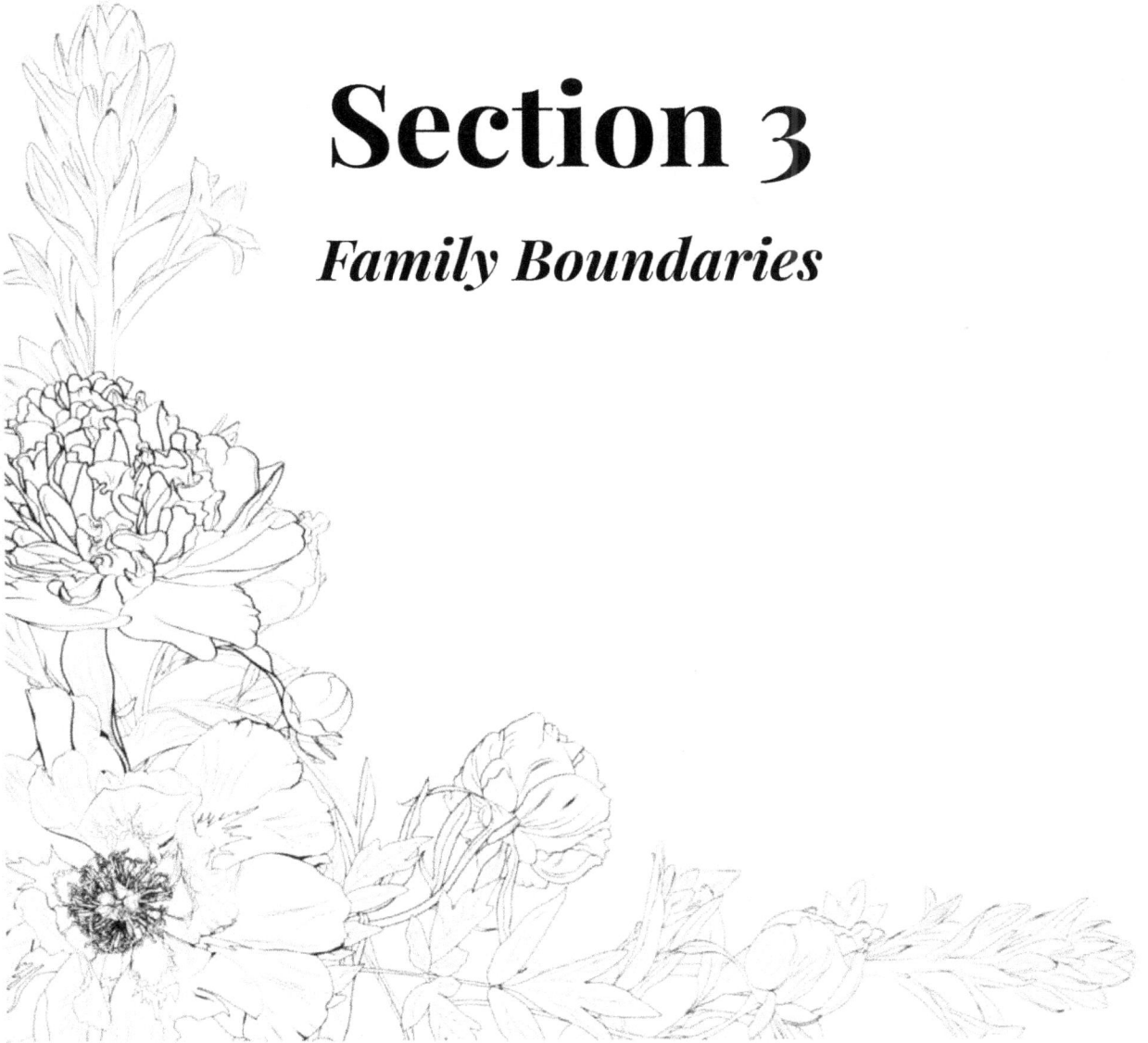

*"You deserve the love
you so freely give to others."*

— *Unknown*

Why Family Boundaries
Are Important

Family relationships can be the most complicated connections in our lives. Having strong boundaries in place and enforcing them are important to creating an atmosphere of respect, protecting emotional health and ensuring good communication. Maintaining family boundaries lets each of you develop a strong sense of self and autonomy. It reduces stress and resentment when everyone knows where they stand.

Identifying Boundary Struggles

As a stepmom, boundary-setting is particularly challenging because of the many roles and expectations placed upon us. Feeling and being genuinely confident and comfortable in your role comes from defining it for yourself and setting boundaries to safeguard your needs, beliefs and values.

Without that? It's a struggle! Boundary struggles stepmoms seem to have in common include:

➢ Feeling obligated to take on responsibilities beyond your comfort level

➢ Finding time to yourself or with your partner without feeling guilty

➢ Dealing with an ex-partner who oversteps boundaries in your home

➢ Juggling mixed expectations around holidays, schedules and discipline

Journal Reflection:

What is the hardest part about setting boundaries in my stepfamily?

Have I ever set a boundary that someone ignored? How did I react?

What ONE small step can I take to strengthen my boundaries this week?

Communicating Boundaries with Confidence

*S*etting boundaries is one thing—but communicating them is another. It's normal to feel nervous about stating your needs. However, clear communication is what prevents misunderstandings. Additionally it helps to prevent resentment from building.

Keys to Communicating Boundaries:

➢ Be clear and specific about what it is you need and expect.

➢ Use "I" statements to express your boundaries without blame.

➢ Expect there to be some pushback and resolve to stay firm.

➢ Practice saying "no" without over-explaining your position.

Journal Reflection:

What's ONE boundary I've hesitated to express out loud? Why?

How could I phrase that concern more clearly and assertively?

What would be the worst-case scenario if I hold firm to that boundary?

What would be the best-case scenario if I hold firm to that boundary?

Boundaries for Real-Life Scenarios

When boundary-setting is new to us, we stepmoms may need help finding the right words. The following boundary scripts help overcome hesitation in scenarios common to stepfamily life. Use the extra space to write your own.

How to set boundaries with Your Partner:

"I love being involved but I need us to have time together that doesn't revolve around stepfamily issues."

How to set boundaries with Stepchildren:

"I care about you but I also need personal space. If my door is closed, it means I need time to myself."

How to set boundaries with an Ex-Partner:

"I prefer to communicate about schedules and logistics only. I won't engage in personal conversations."

How to set boundaries with Extended Family:

"We appreciate your advice but we have a system in place now that works well for our household."

Journal Reflection:

Which of those boundary scripts do I need most in my life right now?

How can I adapt it even further so that it feels 100% natural to me?

Time to Flourish: Boundary Role-Play

Imagine a scenario where you need to set a boundary. Write out a dialogue between you and the other person involved. For example, let's imaging you saying: "I can't take on extra household tasks this week. I have a lot on my plate. I'd also appreciate it if we'd split existing duties 50/50." Next you'll anticipate their reaction. Finally, wrap up with a firm but kind response that reinforces your ask of them. Practice makes perfect, stepmom!

YOU (initial ask):

THEM (possible pushback):

YOU (firm but kind reply):

Journal Reflection:

How did it feel to write this out? Which part was the hardest and why?

How could I use and benefit from this kind of practice run going forward?

Boundary Enforcement, Pushback & Guilt

Many stepmoms struggle with maintaining boundaries once they've set them. But why? This is often true when three things occur either all at once or by themselves: What we've asked for is met with resistance, the other person pushes back hard and/or the ask itself instills guilt or fear in us.

Keys to Holding Firm:

♡ Stay firm, even when faced with pushback from others.

♡ Remind yourself why you set that boundary in the first place.

♡ Give yourself an extra dose of self-care after setting a tough boundary.

♡ Seek support from an understanding friend or mentor who gets it.

♡ Journal about the experience and how it's made you feel.

Remember: Setting boundaries in stepfamilies takes time. It needs periodic assessment and adjustment. Having clear expectations upfront will help each of you adjust more easily, preventing misunderstanding and conflict.

Journal Reflection:

What's ONE boundary that I've let slide again and again? Why?

What steps will I take to reinforce that boundary moving forward?

How do I typically react when someone challenges my boundaries?

What will I do to change that—if anything—moving forward?

Section 4

Boundary Check-ins

"The journey of self-discovery doesn't end with the answers —it begins with the questions we dare to ask ourselves."

-Unknown

Daily and Weekly Boundaries Check-Ins

Small Moments, Big Impact

Setting and maintaining boundaries is an ongoing practice. It's not a one-time decision. Checking in with yourself daily and weekly will help you recognize where your boundaries are working, where they might need some reinforcement and how they seem to be impacting your overall well-being.

Boundaries are a key aspect of self-care. They protect your energy, provide clarity about our relationships with others and ensure that your needs are being met. As a whole, self-care isn't just about indulgences like a Spa Day. It's about making intentional choices which honor the emotional, mental and physical aspects of your health.

This could mean saying "no" to yet another commitment, asking for help when you need it or taking a step back from emotionally taxing interactions. When you prioritize boundary check-ins, you empower yourself to navigate stepfamily dynamics with greater patience, resilience and self-respect. Even small moments of reflection have a big impact.

They're what help you build confidence in your ability to set and uphold boundaries on your way to creating a healthier, more balanced life.

Daily Boundary Check-In

Did I uphold my boundaries today? If not, what made it difficult?

Did I feel guilty about setting a boundary recently? Why or why not?

What's ONE way I made sure to honor my own needs today?

How did enforcing my boundaries impact my energy? My emotions?

Weekly Boundary Check-In

What boundary wins did I have this week?

Where did I struggle with enforcing my boundaries? What made it hard?

Did anyone push back against a boundary I set? If so, how did I handle it?

How can and will I improve my boundary-setting skills moving forward?

What's ONE boundary goal I want to focus on next week?

Section 5

Moving Forward

"*Taking care of yourself doesn't mean 'me first.' It means 'me too.'*"

— L.R. Knost

Closing Reflection

*R*emember that you are deserving of the same love and care that you so generously give to others. The journey of being a stepmother is not always an easy one. It often demands immense courage, patience and emotional strength. Amidst the many challenges and daily sacrifices, never lose sight of your own worth and well-being.

The role you fill, as a stepmom to your partner's children, is both brave and meaningful. Still, I realize that it may not always feel or seem as if your effort is acknowledged by those around you. Yet you're shaping lives, navigating complex family dynamics and pouring your heart into relationships which require unwavering dedication.

These pages are a testament to your journey and a sanctuary where you'll find solace as well as recharge your spirit. Whenever you feel overwhelmed, lost or in need of a reminder of your strength and resilience, return to these words. You'll quickly see that they reflect your experiences, your growth and the incredible person you are.

Beyond the challenges of being a stepmom, remember that you are never alone in this journey. You most definitely are loved, valued and capable of overcoming any obstacle that comes your way. Take care of yourself, being sure to nurture your dreams and aspirations. Never forget how amazing you are and will always be!

Time to Flourish: A Letter to Your Future Self

Write a letter to your future self, describing how you hope to feel about boundary-setting. Imagine reading this a year from now. What will have changed? How will you have shown up for yourself? What do you want to remember most about right now in relation to where you're headed?

Epilogue

Over the many years I've been journaling, I've written letters to myself more times than I can count. What stands out when I read through them now is the hope and willingness I had to change, to grow and to do better. But I'll be honest ...

Those words and thoughts and letters to myself haven't always been easy to revisit, especially if the outcomes I longed for didn't come to pass. What I've come to realize, in the process, is that each one of those moments has been a learning opportunity.

What was I really searching for back then? What am I searching for now in those words I wrote down? What was I hoping to find that felt like it was missing from my life? Looking back, I see that I was trying to figure out who I wanted to become.

And, if I'm really honest with you, I think that continues to be an ongoing process. With every passing year, I grow and evolve. I see the world much differently than I did as a young woman—before I became a stepmom or even a mom. Back then?

I believed I was invincible; capable of anything I wanted and exactly how I wanted. What I didn't account for was how exhausting it is to try to do it all alone. I've since learned that asking for help doesn't make me weak. No, it makes my life easier, more fulfilling and far more enjoyable.

I've learned to let people into my life and not just to orbit around its edges. I've learned to trust those closest to me. And I've learned to set healthy boundaries where I need them most.

Journaling has been one of the most powerful tools in helping me uncover these insights. It still is! While I know that journaling may not instantly feel like the right fit for everyone, I also know that finding support (whether through therapy, coaching or a trusted guide) can be life-changing. For me, it's even been life-saving.

What matters most is discovering what works best for you. Counseling, coaching and journaling are just some of the tools available to help you figure out who you are and what you want from this life you're building. If you're ready to explore all of the possibilities, I'd love to help you create the kind of life and relationships you desire.

It's not only possible. It's absolutely doable! When you're ready, let's connect. Explore "Coach w/me" at StepmomCoach.com to learn about my coaching style and the types of results you might expect from the two of us working together. Scroll down and you'll find a link to my calendar plus an offer for a FREE 30-Min. Consult. Answer a few simple questions to start the process.

If what you want is to create the version of stepfamily life you've hoped for, I know I can help. If this journal has sparked thoughts, insights or moments of reflection, I'd love to hear about them from you. Take a minute to email me directly: Claudette@StepmomCoach.com. In closing, I want to thank you for letting me play a part in your stepmom journey.

- CLAUDETTE

About Claudette

CLAUDETTE CHENEVERT knows the emotional complexity and invisible weight that come with navigating stepfamily life. She's spent 20+ years helping other women find their voices, set healthy boundaries and build stronger relationships. Known worldwide as The Stepmom Coach, she's a trusted guide to those seeking clarity, confidence and peace in their lives and brings deep reserves of lived experience to her work. She's authored:

- ♡ *The Stepmom's Book of Boundaries: How and Where to Draw the Line—for a Happier, Healthier Stepfamily*
- ♡ *Words of Hope, Inspiration and Wisdom for Stepmoms: A Little Extra TLC for the Days that Seem to Be the Hardest*
- ♡ Companion card deck to *The Stepmom's Book of Boundaries*
- ♡ *Claudette Chenevert's 31 Days to Better Communication*

Claudette holds a degree in the psychology of communication with special emphasis on stepfamily dynamics and conflict resolution. Beyond being an ongoing contributor to *StepMom Magazine*, she also hosts and produces the Stepfamily Summit each year as a way to bring together leading voices and lessons from the frontlines of the stepfamily community.

Providing encouragement and helping others embrace their true worth are hallmarks of her approach to working with stepmoms and stepcouples in person and virtually. In all she does, Claudette's mission remains: To help stepmoms go from feeling overwhelmed and uncertain to feeling infinitely more confident, calm and connected. Visit her at StepmomCoach.com.

Stepmom Resources

CLAUDETTE CHENEVERT, aka The Stepmom Coach, is a stepmom and a mom who dedicates herself to helping other women find their authentic voices, set healthier boundaries and build stronger relationships so that they thrive! Her affirmation card deck sparks meaningful conversation and offers daily encouragement. Explore all of the resources available to you online.

Stepmom Boundaries Bundle

ORDER HERE

www.stepmomcoach.com/shop

Remember: As a dedicated member of your family, you deserve clarity, confidence and peace of mind. (Ask Claudette how to achieve all three!)

Additional Resources available here:

Scan to join a supportive community created just for stepmoms.
Connect with women who understand the challenges you're navigating, get practical tools, and access guidance to help you feel more grounded and confident in your daily life.

Join the

Stepmom Coach Community

Scan to receive weekly insights, stories, and stepmom guidance straight to your inbox.
Stay encouraged with practical tips, mindset shifts, and resources to help you navigate your role with clarity, strength, and compassion.

Join the

Stepmom Coach Wisdom Circle

PERSONAL NOTES

www.ingramcontent.com/pod-product-compliance
Lightning Source LLC
Chambersburg PA
CBHW080051280326
41934CB00014B/3279